FLINTSHIRE TOWNS

CONNAH'S QUAY · HOLYWELL · MOLD

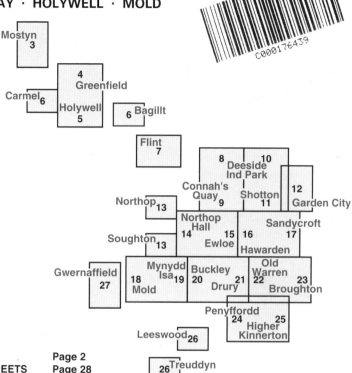

C000176439

Mostyn
3

4
Greenfield

Carmel 6

Holywell
5

6 Bagillt

Flint
7

8   10
Deeside
Ind Park

Connah's
Quay 9

Shotton
11

12

Garden City

Northop 13

Northop
Hall

14   15   16

Ewloe

Sandycroft

17

Soughton 13

Hawarden

Gwernaffield
27

Mynydd
Isa 19

18

Mold

Buckley
20   21
Drury

Old
Warren
22   23
Broughton

Penyffordd
24   25
Higher
Kinnerton

Leeswood 26

ROAD MAP   Page 2
INDEX TO STREETS   Page 28

26 Treuddyn

Every effort has been made to verify
the accuracy of information in this
book but the publishers cannot accept
responsibility for expense or loss
caused by an error or omission.
Information that will be of assistance
to the user of the maps will be welcomed.

The representation on these maps of a
road, track or path is no evidence of the
existence of a right of way.

Car Park	P
Public Convenience	C
Place of Worship	+
One-way Street	→
Pedestrianized	▨
Post Office	●

Scale of street plans 4 inches to 1 mile
Unless otherwise stated

Street plans prepared and published by ESTATE PUBLICATIONS, Bridewell House,
TENTERDEN, KENT, and based upon the ORDNANCE SURVEY mapping with the permission
of The Controller of H. M. Stationery Office.

The Publishers acknowledge the co-operation of the local authorities
of towns represented in this atlas.

© Estate Publications 495 D   ISBN 0 86084 998 8   © Crown Copyright 398713

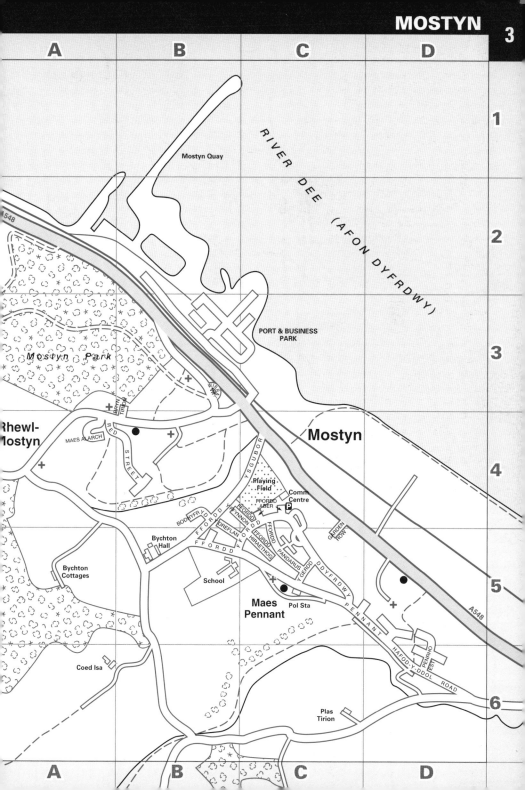

A   B   C   D

1

2

3

4

5

6

River Dee (Afon Dyfrdwy)

Mostyn Quay

A548

Mostyn Park

PORT & BUSINESS PARK

Rhewl-Mostyn

MAES ALARCH

BRYN TIRION

RED STREET

Mostyn

Y SGUBOR

Playing Field

Comm Centre

FFORDD ABER

BODWFR

FFORDD

DREFLAN

FFYNNON

FFORDD HIRAETHOG

FFORDD DD

FFORDD PANDARUS

Y GERDD

GARDEN ROW

Bychton Hall

FFORDD

School

Bychton Cottages

Maes Pennant

Pol Sta

FFORDD DYFRDWY

PENNANT

HAFOD-Y-DDOL

PENRHO EST

PENRHO ROAD

A548

Coed Isa

Plas Tirion

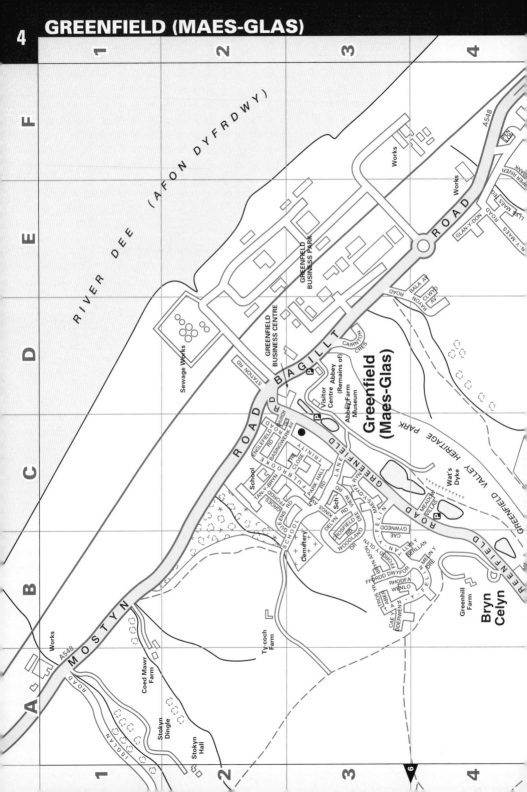

CARMEL & HOLWAY

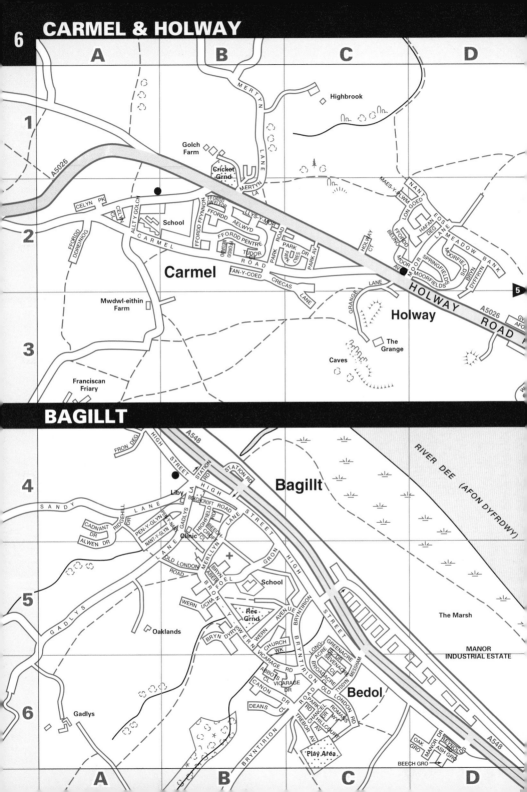

	A	B	C	D

1

Highbrook

MERTYN LANE

Golch Farm

A5026

Cricket Grnd

MERTYN LA

MAES-Y-FLWM LANE

NANT

2

CELYN PK

CELYN

ALLT-Y-GOLCH

CARMEL

School

FFORDD FFYNNON

FFORDD WELED

FFORDD AELWYD

LLYS-Y-MOR

FFORDD PENTRE

TUDOR

ROAD

PARK ROAD

PARK AV

PARK CRES

PARK DR

HOLWAY CT

LON GOED

FFORDD BRONO

HAFAN DEG

EOS

LANE

MEADOW BANK

SPRINGFIELDS

MOORFIELDS

MOORFIELD

BRYN DYFFRYN

FFORDD DYREINIOG

Carmel

TAN-Y-COED

CRECAS LANE

GRANGE LANE

MOOR AV

HOLWAY

ROAD

A5026

GV

AFO

5

Mwdwl-eithin Farm

Holway

The Grange

3

Caves

Franciscan Friary

W

BAGILLT

	A	B	C	D

FRON DEG

HIGH STREET

A548

STATION RD

STATION RD

Bagillt

RIVER DEE (AFON DYFRDWY)

4

SANDY

RIDGEHILL DR

GADLYS LANE

Liby

BEECHCROFT ROAD

HIGHFIELD CROFT

BEECH LANE

HIGH STREET

GRON RD

CADNANT DR

ALWEN DR

PEN-Y-GLYN

NANT-Y-GLYN

Clinic

OLD LONDON ROAD

MERLLYN LANE

BRYN ROEL

ABER

B5121

5

GADLYS

WERN UCHAN

WERN

Rec Grnd

AVENUE

BRYNTIRION

HIGH STREET

School

The Marsh

MANOR INDUSTRIAL ESTATE

Oaklands

BRYN DYRYSW

WERN

CHURCH WK

VICARAGE RD

BRYNTIRION

LONG ACRE

GREENACRE

ACRE

SEVENACRE

BROADACRE

OLD LONDON RD

TYDDYN MESSHAM

Bedol

6

Gadlys

ABBOTS CL

CANON

VICARAGE DR

DEANS CL

ROMANS

PARK GRO

HILLCOURT

AV

TREBOR AV

OAK GRO

MANOR DR

ASH GRO

REYNOLDS

BRYNTIRION

Play Area

BEECH GRO

A548

	A	B	C	D

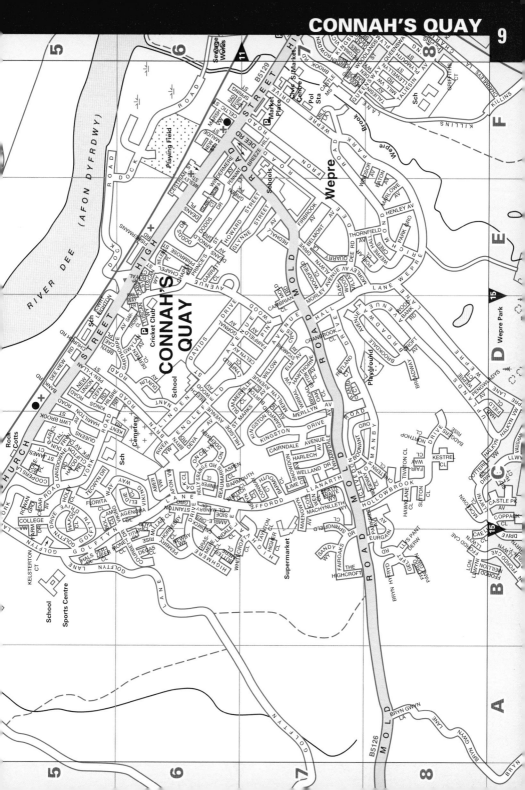

A B C D

SHOTWICK A548 ROAD

A550

GREEN LANE WEST

1

FOURTH AVENUE

SECOND AVENUE

FIRST

DRIVE A
DRIVE B
DRIVE C
DRIVE D

ROAD

GREEN

10

**Deeside
Industrial Park**

FIRST

P
A
R
K

THIRD AV

AVENUE

AVENUE

DROME

ROAD

Sports Ground

LANE

2

RAF SEALAND

DEESIDE
INDUSTRIAL ESTATE

EAST

3

RAF SEALAND

Old Marsh
Farm

GARDEN CITY
INDUSTRIAL ESTATE

HAWTHORNE AVENUE

DEVA
BUSINESS PARK

WELSH ROAD

4

**Garden
City**

CEDAR AV

SEALAND ROAD

SANDY

MAPLE
WOOD AV

DEE RD

Willow
Farm

11

ROAD

QUEENS

VIEW

DEE
LANE

STAFFORD
RD

Playing
Field

ORCHARD

Pol Sta

BRIDGE
SIDLEY D

BY-PASS

A494

SEALAND

VILLA RD

ROAD

A54

ROAD

STONELEIGH
CL

RIVERSIDE

PARK

MANOR

MEADOW VW

5

Scbo

GLEN
FOX

WELSH

AVENUE

WESTON
CLAREMONT

A494

QUEENSFERRY

LANE

MANOR

NORTH
GREEN

SOUTH
GREEN

EAST GREEN

Ferrybank
Farm

Sealand Manor

6

RIVER DEE

rks

A B C 17 D

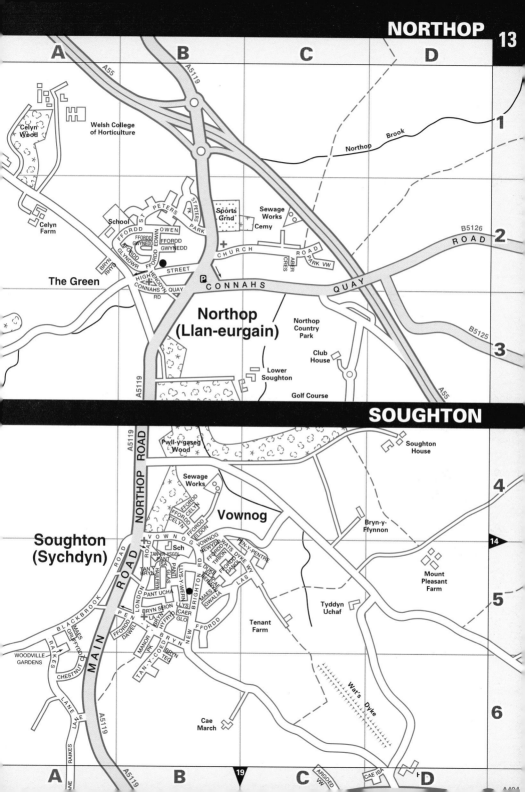

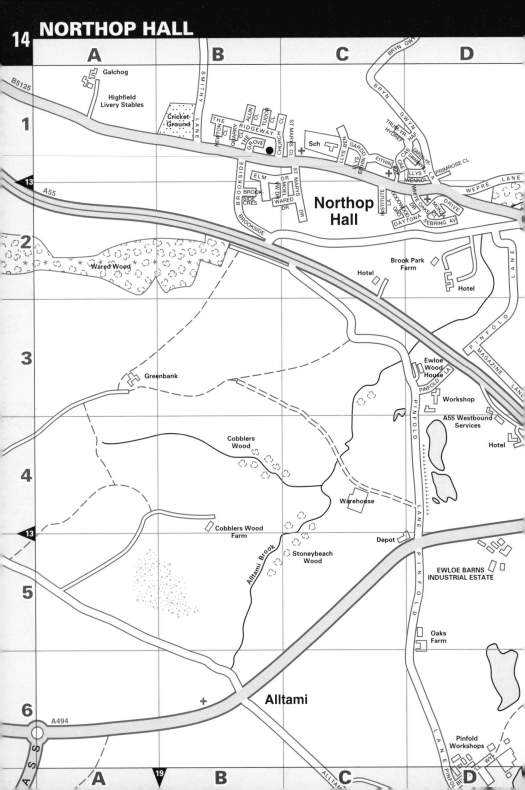

Galchog

Highfield
Livery Stables

B5125

Cricket
Ground

SMITHY LANE

THE
QUARRY
ALLUN CL
RIDGEWAY
TUDOR CL
THE GROVE
NEWTON CL
CHURCH CL
ST MARYS CL

BRYN GWY

BRYN GWYN

Sch

LLYS BEN
GARDD
EITHIN
ELLYS
TRUM YR
HYDREF
HAF
LE
GARDE YR
CA GWAINY

PRIMROSE CL

WEPRE LANE

BROOKSIDE

ELM
DR
WV DR
WARED
DR
ST MARYS DR
MODEL
WARED

BROOK-
SIDE CRES

BROOKSIDE

A55

Northop
Hall

INSTITUTE LA
WOODWARD GRO
WHITE OAKS DR
MONA
DAYTONA
SEBRING AV

PINFOLD LANE

MAGAZINE LANE

Wared Wood

Hotel

Brook Park
Farm

Hotel

Hotel

Greenbank

Ewloe
Wood
House

Workshop

PINFOLD

A55 Westbound
Services

Hotel

Cobblers
Wood

Cobblers Wood
Farm

Alltami Brook

Warehouse

Stoneybeach
Wood

Depot

PINFOLD LANE

EWLOE BARNS
INDUSTRIAL ESTATE

13

Oaks
Farm

Alltami

A494

A55

PINFOLD LANE

Pinfold
Workshops

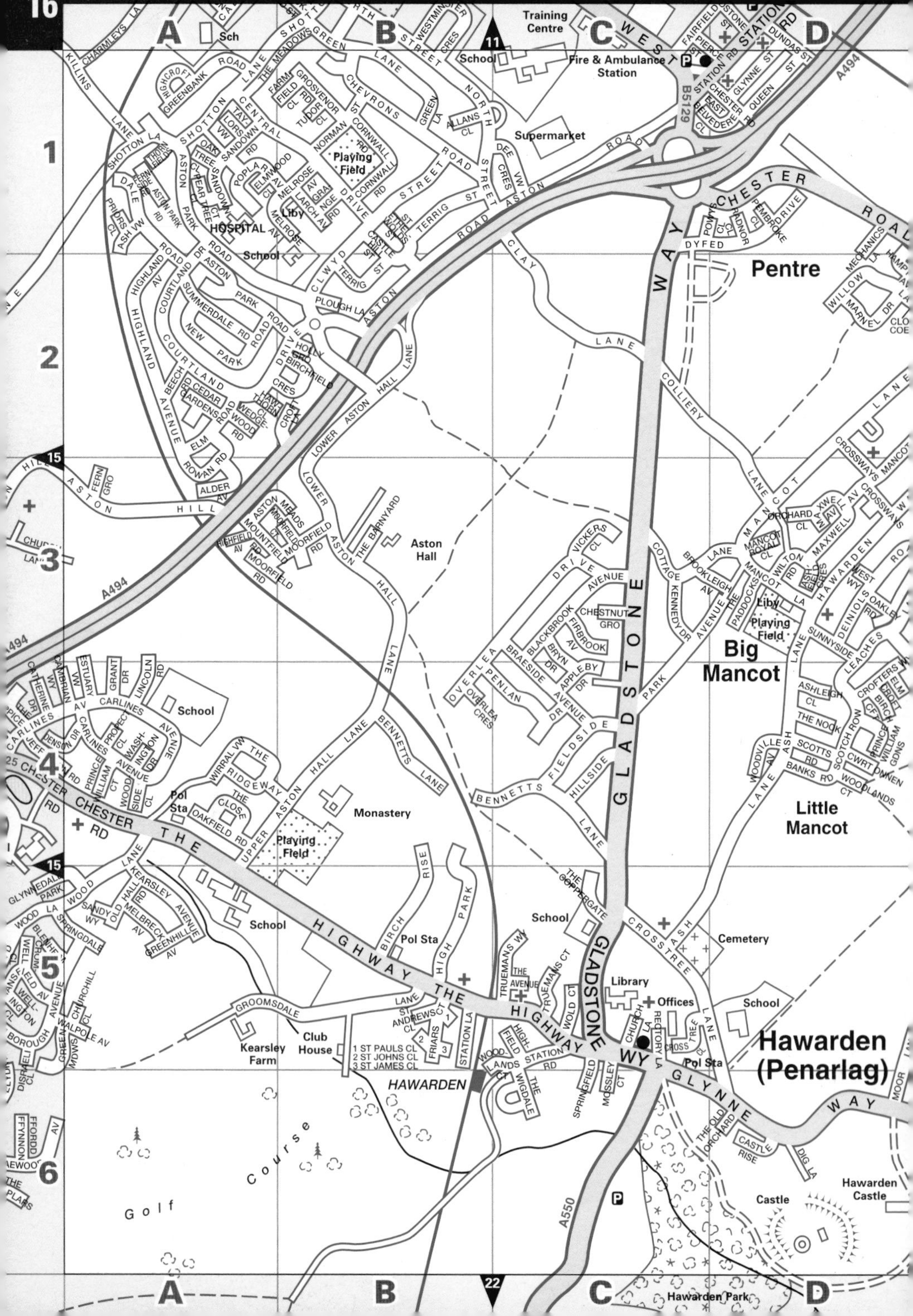
A
B
C
D
1
2
3
4
5
6
11
15
22
Training Centre
School
Fire & Ambulance Station
Supermarket
Sch
Playing Field
Liby
HOSPITAL
Pentre
Aston Hall
School
Big Mancot
Little Mancot
Monastery
Pol Sta
Playing Field
School
Cemetery
Library
Offices
School
Hawarden (Penarlag)
Kearsley Farm
Club House
HAWARDEN
1 ST PAULS CL
2 ST JOHNS CL
3 ST JAMES CL
Golf Course
Castle
Hawarden Castle
Hawarden Park
A494
A550
B5129
GLADSTONE WAY
CHESTER RD
ASTON HILL
THE HIGHWAY
GLYNNE WAY
SHOTTON LA
HIGHLAND AV
COURTLAND DR
ASTON PARK RD
PLOUGH LA
CLAY LANE
COLLIERY LANE
MANCOT LANE
LOWER ASTON HALL LANE
UPPER ASTON HALL LANE
BENNETTS LANE
CROSS TREE LANE
STATION RD
WEST

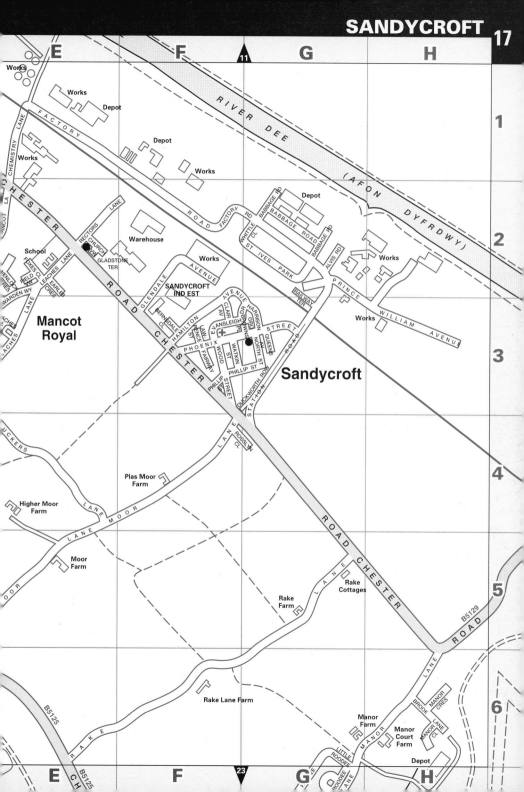

E F 11 G H

1

Works

Works

Depot

Depot

Works

RIVER DEE

(AFON DYFRDWY)

2

CHEMISTRY LANE

FACTORY LANE

Works

CHESTER ROAD

ROAD

FACTORY

Warehouse

Depot

BABBAGE RD

BABBAGE ROAD

BABBAGE RD

WHITTLE RD

ST IVES PARK

ST IVES CL

ALVIS RD

Depot

Works

School

RECTORS LANE

CHURCH VIEW

GLADSTONE TER

LANE

Works

SANDYCROFT IND EST

AVENUE

GLENDALE

BERNEDALE

HAMILTON

CLAIR AV

AVENUE

WOOD ST

PHOENIX

PHILLIP STREET

FAIRWAY

VANSLEIGH

LAWRENCE

HARRISON GRO

ROBBINS WY

WATKIN ST

NORTH ST

QUEENS STREET

PHILLIP ST

DUCKWORTH ROW

STATION

ROAD

RAILWAY

PRINCE WILLIAM AVENUE

Works

Mancot Royal

FIELD VW

FOXES CL

LEACHES LANE

MENLOVE CRES

WARDEN WY

EARLES CRES

LEACHES

CHESTER ROAD

Sandycroft

3

TUCKERS LANE

ROSSLYN CL

4

LANE MOOR

LANE MOOR

Plas Moor Farm

Higher Moor Farm

Moor Farm

CHESTER ROAD

Rake Farm

Rake Cottages

LANE

B5129

ROAD

5

MOOR

B5125

RAKE

Rake Lane Farm

Manor Farm

Manor Court Farm

MANOR LANE

BROOK LANE

MANOR CRES

MANOR CL

Depot

6

E

B5125

CH

F 23 G H

LITTLE ROODEE

ROODEE LANE

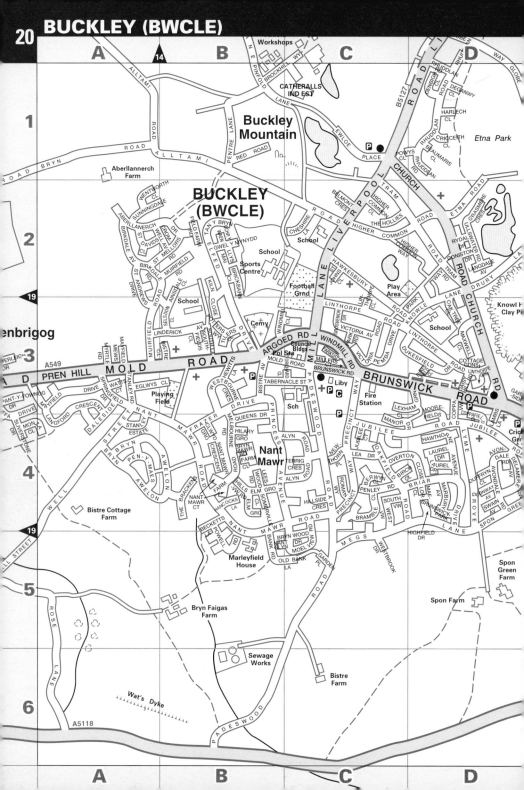

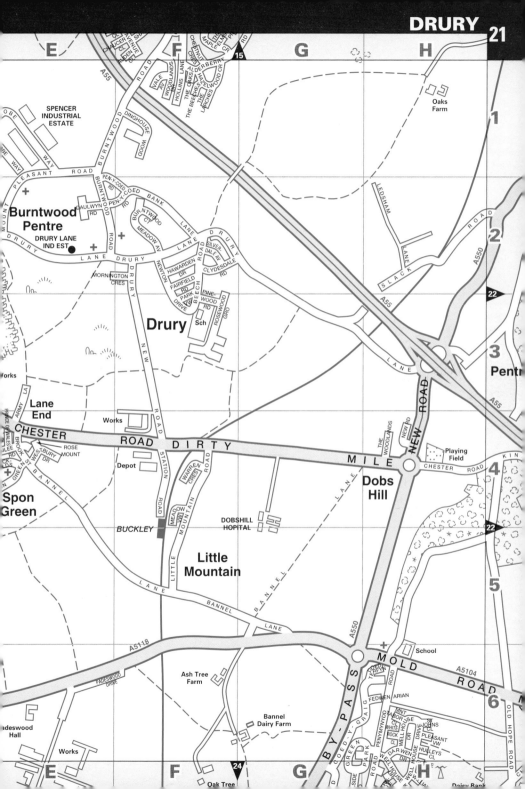

E   F   G   H

15

1

2

22

3

4

22

5

6

Oaks Farm

SPENCER INDUSTRIAL ESTATE

Burntwood Pentre

DRURY LANE IND EST

Burntwood Road

Dinghouse Wood

PEN-Y-COED BANK

DAULWYN RD

PEN-Y-COED

MEADOW AV

NEWTON

MORNINGTON CRES

DRURY LANE

NEW ROAD

HAWARDEN DR

FAIRFIELD

PARK DRIVE

BEECH RD

PINE WOOD RD

SILVER DALE AV

CLYDESDALE RD

ROSEWOOD GRO

DRURY

Sch

Drury

LEDSHAM ROAD

SLACK LANE

A55

CHAUCER AVENUE

QUEEN'S RD

VALE RD

WOODLANDS

HOLLINS LANE

MAPLE

ELM

CR

THE OAKS

ALDERBERRY

THE BEECH

ELYWOOD CR

THE LARCHES

A55

Pentr

LANE

NEW ROAD

NEW RD

THE WOODLANDS

Playing Field

CHESTER ROAD

KIN

Lane End

CHESTER ROAD   DIRTY   MILE

ROSE MOUNT

WESTBURY DR

ARMY LA

BROOK

GREEN ST

BANNEL

Works

Depot

STATION ROAD

WARREN CRES

MEADOW MOUNTAIN ROAD

Dobs Hill

DOBSHILL HOPITAL

Spon Green

BUCKLEY

LITTLE MOUNTAIN LANE

Little Mountain

BANNEL LANE

BANNEL

A5118

PADESWOOD DRIVE

Ash Tree Farm

Bannel Dairy Farm

adeswood Hall

Works

A550

BY-PASS

COED-Y-GRAIG

GREEN PARK ROAD

SIDE

MOLD ROAD

A5104

School

TY FEDWEN ARIAN

PENMYNYDD

DAR WEN

WELL HO

WHITE HO

ROCK HO

MNT

TABOR HO

ST JOHNS CL

CL PLEASANT VW

HURLEYS CL

OLD HOPE ROAD

Oak Tree

24

Daisy Bank

E   F   G   H

A B C D

16

Hawarden Park

Top Park

Beeches Wood

CHESTER ROAD

B5125

A550

ROAD

A550

21

CHERRY

Bilberry Wood

Fishpond Wood

Cherry Orchard Farm

ORCHARD ROAD

Park Farm

Pentrobin

A55

Orchard House

Old Warren

laying Field

KINNERTON OLD ROAD

THE

WARREN

21

+

PENNY BANK

THORNHILL

CHERRY CL

WARREN HALL CT

Warren Hall

LESTERS LANE

KINNERTON OLD RD

KINNERTON OLD ROAD

ROAD

MOLD ROAD

Gravelhole Wood

A5104

ROAD

MOLD ROAD

MOLD

OLD HOPE ROAD

CHESTER ROAD

KINNERTON LANE

Brook Cottages

25

A B C D

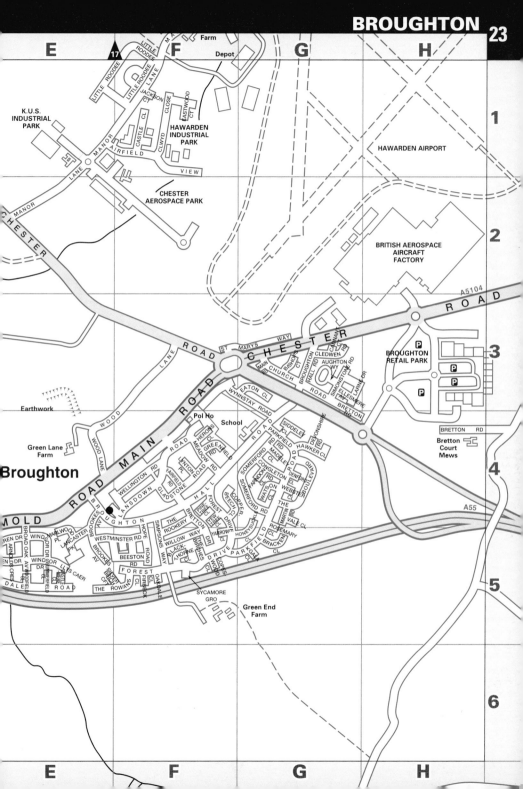

E F G H

1

2

3

4

5

6

K.U.S. INDUSTRIAL PARK

Farm
Depot

HAWARDEN INDUSTRIAL PARK

HAWARDEN AIRPORT

CHESTER AEROSPACE PARK

BRITISH AEROSPACE AIRCRAFT FACTORY

A5104 ROAD

CHESTER ROAD

BROUGHTON RETAIL PARK

Earthwork

Green Lane Farm

BRETTON RD

Bretton Court Mews

Broughton

Pol Ho
School

A55

THE ROOKERY

Green End Farm

SYCAMORE GRO

LITTLE ROODEE
LITTLE ROODEE LANE
JACKSON CT
CASTLE CL
CLWYD
EASTWOOD CT
CLOSE
MANOR
AIRFIELD
VIEW

CHESTER
MANOR LANE

ST MARYS WAY
MAIN LANE ROAD
CHURCH
BISHOPS CT
CLEDWEN
BROUGHTON HALL RD
AUGHTON WY
SIMONSTONE RD
ELLESMERE
LARNE DR
BRETTON

EATON CL
WYNNSTAY ROAD
MEADOW RD
GREENFIELD
HERONS
SIDDELEY
DEVONSHIRE
HAWKER CL
PARKFIELD RD
SOMERFORD RD
MACKIE RD
CONGLETON RD
HANDON RD
WATSON RD
WEBSTER RD
DENFORD RD
TROLLEY RD
COPPER
BEECH CL
BRACKEN CL
ROSEMARY CL
THE VALE CL
MARTIN'S
PARKFIELD
YARROW
HONEY'S
FOREST DRIVE
DRIVE
BIRCHES
BLACKTHORNE WAY
WILLOW WAY
SIMPSONS WAY
HOPE ROAD
GLADSTONE
LANSDOWN
WELLINGTON RD
FAIRFIELD PL
LINTON ROAD
HALL RD
WOOD LANE
WOOD

MOLD
ROAD MAIN ROAD
BROUGHTON
BROOKES
WARLWO PL
LANCASTER RD
WINDSOR DR
GOR DR
ARNOLDS CRES
BROAD OAK AV
DALE
WINDSOR DR
SUMMERFIELD DR
LLYS CAER
FOREST
BEESTON RD
WESTMINSTER RD
THE ROWANS
ROAD
SILVER
FIRBECK
OAKDALE

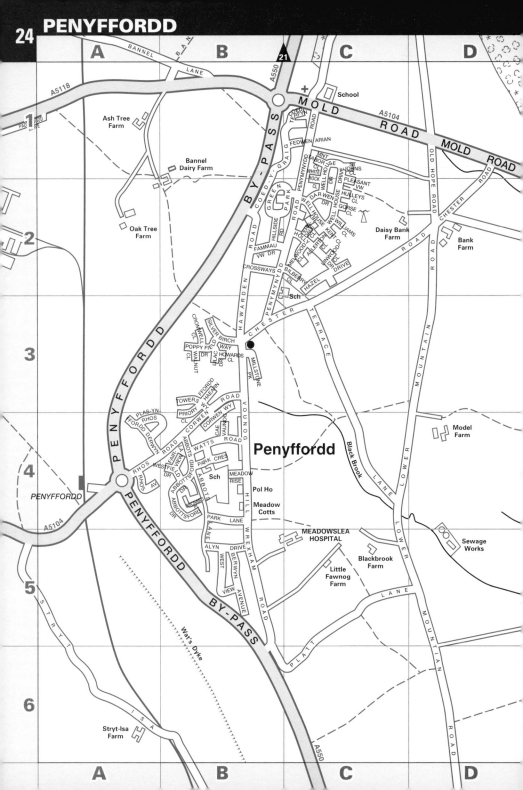

A B C D

BANNEL LANE

A5118

21

MOLD ROAD

A550

School

A5104

MOLD ROAD

Ash Tree Farm

Bannel Dairy Farm

BY-PASS

COED-Y-GRAIG

CREFTYN

FEDWEN ARIAN

PENYMYNYDD

RABOR CL

WHITE ROCK

GRAIG RD

PARK RD

HILLSIDE

MNT

ST JOHNS

PLEASANT

WELL HO

WELL HOUSE

DARWEN DR

WELL HOUSE

GORSE

HULLEYS CL

KENT

WILLIAMS

OLD HOPE ROAD

CHESTER ROAD

Oak Tree Farm

FAMMAU VW DR

CROSSWAYS

MEADOW VW DR

BILBERRY CL

HOPE CL

ALLERTON CL

LINWOOD

HAZEL

DRIVE

Sch

Daisy Bank Farm

Bank Farm

HAWARDEN ROAD

CHESTER ROAD

PENYMYNYDD

TERRACE

CROMWELL CL

SILVER BIRCH WAY

POPPY FIELD

WALNUT CL

HOWARDS CL

MILLSTONE PK

MOUNTAIN ROAD

PENYFFORDD

TOWERS

PLAS-YN-RHOS

FORDD DERWYN

LEFORDD

PRIORY CL

CORWEN CL

HAEARN

CORWEN WY

CAE VAUNOG

YOUNG ROAD

Penyffordd

Black Brook

LOWER

Model Farm

RHOS AV

RHOS

WESTFIELD

FAIRWAY

ABBOTTSFORD DR

WATTS

PARK CRES

Sch

MEADOW RISE

HILL

WREXHAM ROAD

Pol Ho

Meadow Cotts

MEADOWSLEA HOSPITAL

Blackbrook Farm

Little Fawnog Farm

LOWER LANE

MOUNTAIN

Sewage Works

PENYFFORDD

PENYFFORDD BY-PASS

A5104

ABBOTS FORD DR

PARK LANE

PARK AVE

ALYN

BERWYN AVENUE

DRIVE

WEST VIEW

PLATT

A550

War's Dyke

STRYT ISA

Stryt-Isa Farm

MOUNTAIN ROAD

A B C D

1 2 3 4 5 6

E   F   G   H

1

2

3

4

5

6

WARREN HALL CT

Warren Hall

Gravelhole Wood

MOLD ROAD

KINNERTON OLD RD

LESTERS LANE

Brook Cottages

Bramley Hall Farm

KINNERTON LANE

Mount Farm

Kinnerton Lodge

LESTERS LANE

Bramley Farm

BRAMLEY LANE

Bramley Lane Farm

Crompton Hall Farm

LLYS DERWEN

LLYS HUNERS

CROFT

FOXES WK

THE CHASE

School

DEANSWAY

OAK DR

SPRINGFIELD CL

MYRTLE AV

GREENFIELD

The Grange

LANE

ROAD

Higher Kinnerton

PARK AV

CROMPTON CL

Playing Field

KIRKET AVENUE

MAIN ROAD

MEADOWCROFT

WILL CT

MAIN ROAD

PADDOCK WY

BENNETTS WAY

BLANTERN RD

BEESTON RD

Kinnerton Hall Farm

HART LEY

BURTON DR

ECCLESTON RD

KINNERTON HEIGHTS

FAULKNERS CL

SANDY LANE

Babylon

CANNON

GREEN LANE

Bradbrook Farm

KINNERTON LANE

The Dale

Sandy Lane Farm

SANDY LANE

Kinnerton Bank Farm

E   F   G   H

22

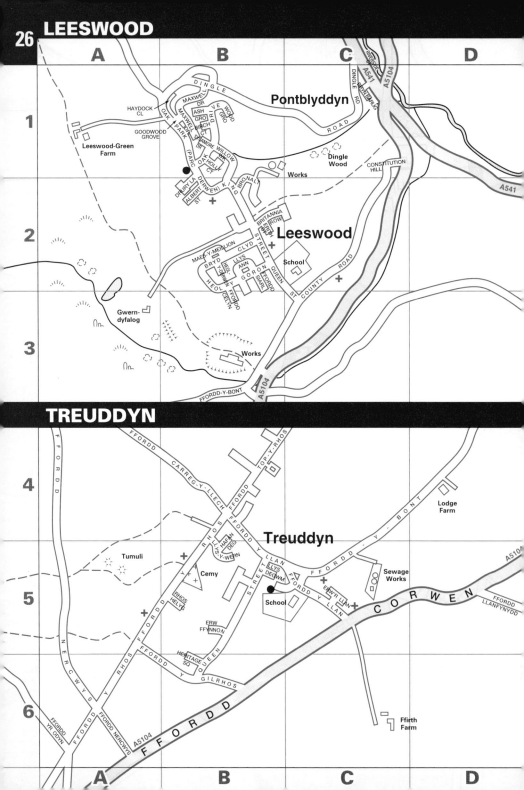

LEESWOOD

A · B · C · D

1 · 2 · 3

HAYDOCK CL
Leeswood-Green Farm
GOODWOOD GROVE
DINGLE
MAXWELL DR
ASH GRO
BIRCH GRO
DRIVE WOOD
VE GRO
OAK PARK
MAXWELL DR
WILLOW DR
OAK HOLLY
(PARC
OAK CT
DRURY LA
ALBERT ST
DERWEN JL
KING
BRONALT
BRITANNIA
ROW
Pontblyddyn
ROAD
Works
Dingle Wood
CONSTITUTION HILL
A541
A5104
A541

Leeswood

MAES-Y-MEILLION
BRYD
HEOL ANN
LLYS
CLYD
GORON
SARL
FFORDD
HEOL CEILYN
QUEEN ST
STREET
County
School
ROAD
Gwern-dyfalog
Works
FFORDD-Y-BONT
A5104

TREUDDYN

A · B · C · D

4 · 5 · 6

FFORDD
FFORDD
CARREG-Y-LLECH
TOP-Y-RHOS
FFORDD
RHOS
LLYS-Y-WERN
HAFAN DEG
FFORDD LLAN
Lodge Farm
FFORDD-Y-BONT
A5104

Treuddyn

Tumuli
Cemy
LLYS DEGWM
ERW LLAN
Sewage Works
RHOS HELYG
School
FFORDD Y LLAN
CORWEN
FFORDD LLANFYNYDD
ERW FFYNNON
HERITAGE SQ
FFORDD Y QUEEN
GILRHOS
NERCWYS
Ffirth Farm
FFORDD YR ODYN
FFORDD NERCWYS
A5104
FFORDD

A   B   C   D

1

2

3

4

5

6

ROAD

GWERNAFFIELD ROAD

ROAD

RHYD Y MWYN

LWYN Y BEDW

CAE RHUG LANE

Gwernaffield

Sch

School

TAI NESTIGA
CHURCH LA
MAES Y LLAN
CAER

Y-WAEN

MUD

BWLCH-Y-DDEU-FRYN

GWERNAFFIELD

THE LINKS

TAN-Y-

Y-HAFOD

Cemetery †

HGH PARK

Golf
ourse

Downhill
Quarry

Cefn Mawr
Quarry

HAFOD

Fron-yw

ROAD

HAFOD

GODRE'R COED

UWCH-Y-DRE

UWCH-Y-DRE

GODRE'R
MYNYDD

NEOL-Y-WERN

CAE-Y-
LLAN

GODRE'R COED

Sch

BLAEN WERN

HAFOD
Y-WERN

Cadole

Country
Park

ROAD

SWAN LANE

Sch †

494

R U T H I N

ROAD

R U T H I N

Gwernymynydd

A494

MINE FFORDD
RELESS

ROAD

BRYN EITHIN

BRYN
ETHIN

CLYS
FANS

G L Y N D W R

ROAD

A   B   C   D

The Index includes some names for which there is insufficient space on the maps. These names are preceded by an * and are followed by the nearest adjoining thoroughfare.

BAGILLT

Abbots Cl CH6   6 B6
Alwen Dr CH6   6 A5
Ash Gro CH6   6 D6
Beech Gro CH6   6 C5
Beechcroft CH6   6 B4
Beechcroft Cl CH6   6 B4
Broadacre Cl CH6   6 C6
Bron-y-Wern CH6   6 B5
Bryn Aber CH6   6 B5
Bryn Dyrys CH6   6 B5
Bryntirion CH6   6 C5
Bryntirion Rd CH6   6 B6
Cadnant Dr CH6   6 A4
Canon Dr CH6   6 C6
Chancel Dr CH6   6 C6
Church Walk CH6   6 C5
Deans Cl CH6   6 B6
Foel Gron CH6   6 B5
Fron Deg CH6   6 A4
Gadlys La CH6   6 C5
Greenacre Dr CH6   6 C5
High St CH6   6 A4
Highfield Rd CH6   6 B4
Hillcourt Av CH6   6 C6
INDUSTRIAL & RETAIL:
Manor Industrial Est CH6   6 D6
Longacre Dr CH6   6 C5
Manor Dr CH6   6 D6
Merllyn La CH6   6 B5
Nant-y-Glyn CH6   6 A5
Oak Gro CH6   6 D6
Old London Rd CH6   6 B5
Old London Rd,
  Bedol CH6   6 C6
Park Rd CH6   6 C6
Pen-y-Glyn CH6   6 A4
Pen-y-Nant CH6   6 B4
Reynolds Rd CH6   6 D6
Ridgehill Dr CH6   6 A4
Romans Way CH6   6 C6
Sandy La CH6   6 A4
Sevenacre Cl CH6   6 C6
Station Rd CH6   6 B4
Trebor Av CH6   6 C6
Tyddan Messham CH6   6 C6
Vicarage Rd CH6   6 B6
Vicarage Rd CH6   6 B5
Wern Av CH6   6 B5
Wern Ucha CH6   6 B5

CONNAH'S QUAY / MOLD / BUCKLEY

Abbots La CH4   24 B4
Abbottsford Dr CH4   24 B4
Aber Cres CH7   13 C2
Aber Vw CH5   9 C6
Aberllanerch Dr CH7   20 A2
Acacia Cl CH7   18 B5
Ael-y-Bryn CH7   18 B5
Afon Vw CH5   9 C6
Agenora Cl CH5   9 C6
Ainsdale CH7   20 B3
Airfield Rd CH4   23 F4
Airfield Vw CH4   23 E1
*Albert Pl,
  Fishermans Rd CH5   9 E6
Albert St CH7   26 B2
Alder Av CH5   16 A3
Alderberry Rd CH7   21 F1
*Aled Ho,
  Lakeside Business Village CH5   15 G5
Alexandra Rd CH7   18 C5

Alexandra St CH5   11 A7
Allans Cl CH5   16 B1
Allerton Cl CH4   24 C2
Alltami Rd CH7   20 A1
Alun Cl CH7   14 B1
Alvis Rd CH5   17 G2
Alwen Av CH5   19 G3
Alwyn Cl CH7   18 B2
Alwyn Dr CH5   9 E7
Alyn Dale Av CH7   19 G4
Alyn Dr CH4   24 B5
Alyn Mdw CH7   18 C3
Alyn Pk CH5   15 H6
Alyn Rd CH7   20 C4
Alyn St CH7   18 D3
Ambleside Cl CH5   9 C6
Anfield Cl CH5   15 F1
Appleby Dr CH5   16 C4
Aran Cl CH7   19 G2
Archway CH7   18 D6
Argoed Av CH7   19 E1
Argoed Hall La CH7   19 F3
Argoed Rd CH7   20 B3
Argoed Vw CH7   19 E1
Army La CH7   21 E4
Arnold Gro CH7   9 E6
Arnolds Cres CH4   23 E5
Ash Gro,
  Leeswood CH7   26 B1
Ash Gro, Mold CH7   18 B3
Ash Gro,
  Mynydd Isa CH7   19 H3
Ash Gro, Shotton CH5   11 B7
Ash La CH5   16 C5
Ash Vw CH5   16 A1
Ashfield Cres CH5   16 D3
Ashfield Rd CH5   11 B7
Ashleigh Cl CH5   16 D4
Aspen Cl CH5   9 C6
Aston Hill CH5   15 H3
Aston Meads CH5   16 A3
Aston Park Rd CH5   16 A1
Aston Rd CH5   16 B2
Auden Cl CH5   21 F1
Aughton Way CH4   23 G3
Austen Cl CH5   15 G6
*Avon Ct, Welland Dr,
  Connahs Quay CH8   9 C7
Avon Ct, Mold CH7   18 C5
Avondale CH7   20 D4

Babbage Rd CH5   17 G2
Badgers Rise CH5   9 C8
*Bala Ho,
  Lakeside Business Village CH5   15 G5
Bank La CH7   21 F2
Bank Rd, Buckley CH7   20 B5
Bank Rd,
  Connahs Quay CH5   9 D5
Bank Row CH7   20 D4
Bank Villas CH7   18 C4
Banks Rd CH5   16 D4
Bannel La CH7   21 E4
Barmouth Cl CH5   9 C7
Bartland Gro CH5   11 E7
Beaumaris Cl CH7   20 D1
Beaumaris Rd CH5   9 C6
Becketts La CH7   20 B4
Bedford Way CH7   18 B3
Beech Dr CH7   18 B4
Beech Gro CH7   19 G3
Beech Rd, Drury CH7   21 F3
Beech Rd,
  Shotton CH5   16 A2
Beechwood Av CH5   9 D6
Beechwood Cl CH7   18 B2
Beeston Rd,
  Broughton CH4   23 F5
Beeston Rd,
  Higher Kinnerton CH4   25 H4
Belmont Av CH5   9 E7
Belmont Cres CH7   20 C2
Belvedere Cl CH5   16 C1
Benllech Cl CH5   9 C6
Bennetts La,
  Hawarden CH5   16 B4

Bennetts La,
  Higher Kinnerton CH4   25 G4
Bernsdale Cl CH5   17 F3
Berwyn Av CH4   24 B5
Berwyn Cl,
  Buckley CH7   20 C4
Berwyn Cl,
  Mynydd Isa CH7   19 G2
Bilberry Cl CH4   24 C2
Birch Cft CH5   16 D4
Birch Cl CH7   20 C4
*Birch Ct, Pen-y-Llan,
  Connahs Quay CH8   9 D5
Birch Ct,
  Leeswood CH5   26 B1
Birch Rise CH5   16 B1
Birchfield Cres CH5   16 B2
Birkdale Av CH7   20 A2
Birkdale Rd CH7   20 A2
Bishops Ct CH4   23 G3
Bistre Av CH7   20 B3
Bistre Cl CH7   20 B3
Blackbrook Av CH5   16 C3
Blackbrook Rd CH7   13 A5
Blackthorn Cl CH4   23 F5
Blaen Wern CH7   27 D5
Blantern Rd CH4   25 H4
Blenheim Cl CH5   15 H5
Bod Offa Dr CH7   19 H4
Bodnant Gro CH7   9 C7
Bollam Cl CH5   9 C5
Bracken Cl CH4   23 G5
Braeside Av CH5   16 C3
Bramble Cl CH7   20 C4
Bramley La CH4   25 E4
Bramley Way CH5   15 G5
Breeze Hill CH5   9 F7
*Brenig Ho,
  Lakeside Business Village CH5   15 G5
Bretton Dr CH4   23 F4
Bretton Rd CH4   23 H4
Bretton Rd CH4   23 G3
Briar Dr CH7   20 D4
Brickbarn Ct CH7   20 B2
Brickfields CH7   21 E4
Bridge St, Mold CH7   18 C3
Bridge St,
  Shotton CH5   11 A7
Bridge Vw CH5   11 E7
Britannia Row CH7   26 B2
Bro Alun CH7   18 D5
Broad Oak Av CH4   23 E4
Broad Oak Cl CH5   9 D7
Broadway,
  Connahs Quay CH5   9 D8
Broadway,
  Ewloe CH5   15 G4
Brockhill Way CH7   20 B1
Bromfield Cl CH7   18 D5
Bromfield La CH7   18 D6
Bromfield Pk CH7   18 C5
Bronalt CH7   26 B2
Broncoed La CH7   18 C6
Broncoed Pk CH7   18 C5
Bronte Gro CH15   G 5
Bron-y-Nant CH5   18 D4
Bron-yr-Eglwys CH7   19 H4
Brook La CH4   17 H6
Brook Rd CH5   9 C7
Brook St, Buckley CH7   21 E4
Brook St, Mold CH5   18 C5
Brookdale Av CH5   9 D8
Brooke Cl CH5   15 G5
Brookes Av CH4   23 E5
Brookleigh Av CH5   9 D6
Brookside Cres CH7   14 B2
Brookside,
  Garden City CH5   11 E7
Brookside,
  Northop Hall CH7   14 B2
Broughton Hall Rd CH4   23 E4
Browns Pl CH5   17 F3
Brunswick Pk CH7   20 D4
Brunswick Rd CH7   20 C3
Brunswood Grn CH5   15 H6
Bryd Clyd CH7   26 B2

Bryn Awelon,
  Buckley CH7   20 A4
Bryn Awelon,
  Mold CH7   18 D2
Bryn Barug CH7   26 C1
Bryn Cae Pl CH5   9 D5
Bryn Clwyd CH7   19 F2
Bryn Coch Cres CH7   18 B5
Bryn Coch La CH7   18 B5
Bryn Coed Wepre CH5   15 E1
Bryn Derwen CH7   19 H4
Bryn Dr CH5   16 C3
Bryn Eithin CH7   27 C6
Bryn Garmon CH7   18 B4
Bryn Gwyn La CH7   9 A8
Bryn Heulog CH7   18 B4
Bryn Hilyn La CH7   18 D5
Bryn Hyfryd,
  Connahs Quay CH5   9 B8
Bryn Hyfryd,
  Soughton CH7   13 B5
Bryn Mawr Rd CH7   20 B4
Bryn Oddfa CH7   18 B3
Bryn Offa CH7   19 F4
Bryn Rhyd CH7   13 A2
Bryn Rd, Buckley CH7   20 A1
Bryn Rd,
  Connahs Quay CH5   9 C6
Bryn Rd,
  Mynydd Isa CH7   19 G4
Bryn Rd,
  New Brighton CH7   19 F1
Bryn Seion La CH7   13 B5
*Bryn Seion Ter,
  Bryn Seion La CH7   13 B5
Bryn Teg CH7   13 B5
Bryn Wood Dr CH7   20 B5
Bryn-y-Baal Rd CH7   19 F1
Burns CH5   15 G6
Burntwood Ct CH7   21 F2
Burntwood Rd CH7   21 E1
Burton Cl CH5   9 D7
Burton Dr CH4   25 G4
Butler St CH5   11 A8
Buttermere Cl CH5   9 B6
Bwlch-y-Ddeufryn CH7   27 A2
Byron Cl,
  Connahs Quay CH5   15 F1
Byron Cl, Ewloe CH5   15 G6

Cable St CH5   9 E6
Cadlas Cl CH5   15 E1
Cadnant Ct CH4   23 G3
Cae Berwyn CH7   13 B5
Cae Bracty CH7   18 C4
Cae Glas CH7   18 A5
Cae Haf CH7   14 C1
Cae Hir CH7   18 A4
Cae Isa CH7   19 F1
Cae Llys Cl CH5   9 B8
Cae Rhug La CH7   27 A1
Cae Vaunog CH4   24 B4
Caer Mul CH7   27 B2
Caernarvon Cl CH5   11 A8
Cairndale Av CH5   9 C7
Caldbeck Cres CH5   9 B6
Cambrian Cl,
  Connahs Quay CH5   9 D7
Cambrian Cl,
  Mold CH7   18 D6
Cambrian Way CH5   15 H3
Camrose Cl CH5   15 E1
Cannon Way CH4   25 G4
Canol-y-Bryn CH7   19 G2
Carlines Av CH5   15 H4
Carton Rd CH7   19 G4
Castle Cl CH4   23 F1
Castle Hill St CH5   16 B1
Castle Mews CH5   9 F7
Castle Park Av CH5   15 E1
Castle Rise CH5   16 D6
Castlemere Cl CH5   23 E5
Catherine Dr CH5   15 H4
Cedar Av,
  Connahs Quay CH5   9 C6
Cedar Av,
  Garden City CH5   12 B4

*Cedar Ct,
  Pen-y-Llan CH8   9 D
Cedar Gdns CH5   16 A
Cedar Gro CH7   18 B
Cefn Rd CH5   9 D
Celtic St CH5   9 E
Celyn Av CH5   9 D
Central Dr CH5   16 A
Cestrian St CH5   9 E
Chambers La CH7   19 C
Chapel Ct CH5   9 E
Chapel St,
  Connahs Quay CH5   9 E
Chapel St, Mold CH7   18 C
Charles St CH7   18 C
Charmleys La CH5   16 A
Chaucer St CH5   15 C
Chemistry La CH5   15 E
Cheriton CH5   15 E
Cherry Dale Rd CH4   22 D
Cherry Orchard Rd CH5   22 B
Cheshire La CH7   20 C
Chesnut Cres CH5   15 H
Chester St CH7   18 C
Chester Cl CH5   11 A
Chester Rd East CH5   15 E
Chester Rd West CH5   11 A
Chester Rd,
  Broughton CH4   23 E
Chester Rd,
  Buckley CH5,7   21 E
Chester Rd,
  Ewloe CH5   15 H
Chester Rd, Mold CH7   18 D
Chester Rd,
  Pentre CH5   16 D
Chester Rd,
  Penyffordd CH4   24 H
Chester Rd,
  Sandycroft CH5   17 H
Chesterton Av CH5   15 G
Chestnut Cl CH7   13 A
*Chestnut Ct,
  Pen-y-Llan CH8   9 D
Chestnut Cres CH5   15 H
Chestnut Gro CH5   16 D
Chestnut Rd CH7   18 A
Chevrons Rd CH5   16 B
Chiltern Cl CH5   9 D
Church Cl CH7   14 C
Church La,
  Ewloe CH5   15 H
Church La,
  Gwernaffield CH7   27 B
Church La,
  Hawarden CH5   16 B
Church La, Mold CH7   18 D
Church Rd,
  Broughton CH4   23 C
Church Rd,
  Buckley CH7   20 B
Church Rd,
  Connahs Quay CH5   9 D
Church Rd,
  Northop CH7   13 B
Church St CH5   9 E
Church Vw CH5   17 E
Churchill Cl CH5   16 A
Cilnant CH7   18 A
Circular Dr CH5   15 C
Clair Av CH5   17 H
Claremont Av CH5   11 A
Clarence St CH5   11 A
Clay La CH5   16 B
Clayton Cl CH7   18 A
Clayton Rd CH7   19 C
Cledwen Dr CH7   19 C
Cledwen Rd CH4   23 C
Cleveland Gro CH5   11 H
Clifton Park Av CH5   15 C
Clivedon Rd CH5   9 C
Clos Coed CH5   16 D
Clos Lindum CH7   18 A
Clos-y-Meillion CH5   15 C
Clwyd Av CH7   19 C
Clwyd Cl CH4   23
Clwyd Gro CH7   20 B